All You Need Is Love

The Canadian Brass

T0045059

ISBN 978-0-634-00130-7

EXCLUSIVELY DISTRIBUTED BY

HAL•LEONARD®
CORPORATION
7777 W. BLUEMOUND RD. P.O. BOX 13819 MILWAUKEE, WI 53213

Visit Hal Leonard Online at
www.halleonard.com

All You Need Is Love

Trumpet 1

Words and Music by John Lennon
and Paul McCartney

80
repeat to fade

85

90

95

100

104
faded by now

Blackbird

Words and Music by John Lennon
and Paul McCartney

Trumpet 1

Come Together

Words and Music by John Lennon
and Paul McCartney

Trumpet 1

Eleanor Rigby

Words and Music by John Lennon
and Paul McCartney

Trumpet 1

I Am The Walrus

Words and Music by John Lennon
and Paul McCartney

Trumpet 1

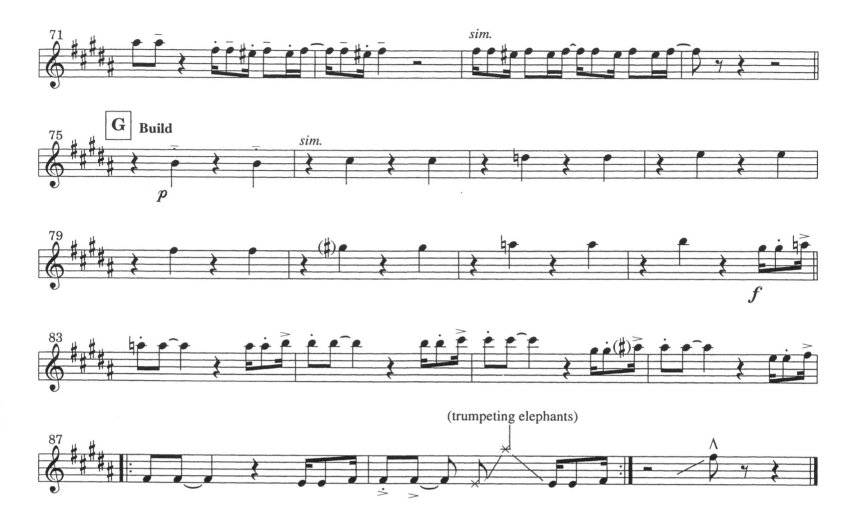

(trumpeting elephants)

She's Leaving Home

Words and Music by John Lennon
and Paul McCartney

Trumpet 1

I Want To Hold Your Hand

Words and Music by John Lennon
and Paul McCartney

Trumpet 1

Michelle

Words and Music by John Lennon
and Paul McCartney

Trumpet 1

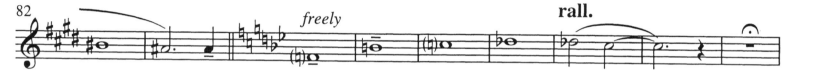

Penny Lane

Words and Music by John Lennon
and Paul McCartney

Piccolo Trumpet

When I'm Sixty-Four

Words and Music by John Lennon
and Paul McCartney

Trumpet 1

With A Little Help From My Friends

Words and Music by John Lennon
and Paul McCartney

Trumpet 1

You Never Give Me Your Money

Words and Music by John Lennon
and Paul McCartney

Trumpet 1

4x's (or repeat to fade)

molto rall.
to Piccolo

Yesterday

Trumpet 1

Words and Music by John Lennon
and Paul McCartney